PUNS IN YOU
VOLUME 2

ANOTHER 101

AMAZING(ISH)

PUNS

By Max Harvey

I was sceptical when they told me I'd won the Crab Fighting Championship.

I took it with a pinch assault.

People think the makers of Campari and Aperol are friends, but they're actually bitter rivals.

- Are you the man whose entire vocabulary is types of arthropod?
- Mite bee.

- One of the Red Arrows missed a display after going home to check his boiler.

- Pilot light?

- Yeah, they were one short.

LOUDEST EVER DONKEY DISCOVERED ON LOCAL FARM

More on this bray king story as we have it.

A rise in unexplained deaths has been blamed on the Ministry of Justice cutting coroners.

I didn't think the new Netflix documentary series, 'Black Holes and Quicksand' would interest me, but I've really got sucked in.

My grandfather produced the first Bombay Sapphire in his loft distillery, and then my father developed Gordon's in his own roof space.

Coincidence, or good gin attics?

I saw an egg and spoon race once. It was rubbish. And the egg only won because the race was on a hill.

Would I greet friends with loud theatrical kisses...?

Mwah?

I don't mind sketching statues in a museum or trees in a park, but I draw the lion at zoos.

My nunchuck skills are whirled beating.

My wig stews are so similar, they're like toupees in a pot.

The motto of the Vanilla Ice School of Dog Obedience is 'Stop, Collie Berate and Listen'.

Dick Van Dyke discovered you could freeze vaccines inside thin lollies and demonstrated it with a friend at a medical conference.

He super-cooled his fragile ice stick expo ally doses.

Doing the splits is now a nationwide obsession, according to widespread reports.

WAITER: I'm afraid the soup is just for Members of Parliament

ME: Minister only?

WAITER: No, carrot and coriander

My chef friend loved it when I whispered "small onion" in his ear.

It meant shallot to him.

There's this cool bar on the corner of Femur Road and Pelvis Avenue.

It's a hip joint.

- Just spoke to a man who tried to sell me an ice pack to hang around my dog's neck.

- Cold collar?

- No, I phoned him.

I got rich working at the blow-up doll factory.

I was making sex figures.

The greatest accolade in journalism is a mystery gift in a cracker, known as the 'pull it' surprise.

I sold some Nostradamus-themed jewellery for inflated prices and got done for prophet earring.

- One of the seven dwarfs is bullying the others.
- Dopey mean?
- I think he does get a buzz from it, yeah.

I'm thinking of studying Christmas Misery at university.

BA Humbug.

Do FTSE companies do their deals under the table?

Brewers have nearly perfected a beer that tastes like Lego.

They're just working out the Technic Ale details.

People are falling over themselves to sign up for my beginner's clown course.

Armstrong went to the moon in 1969, but Superman's nemesis didn't get there till 1980.

Neil before Zod.

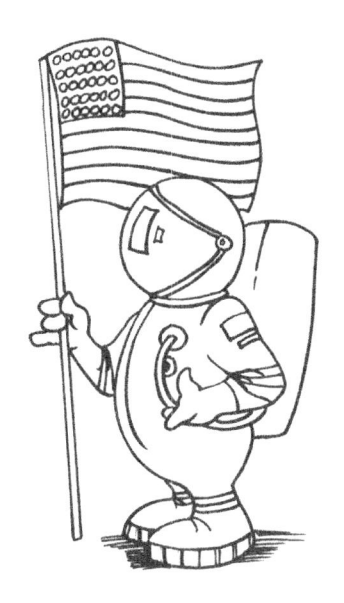

fell in love with a woman who wooed me by singing Beyoncé songs. She had me at Halo.

Is the new Braille pharmacy open?

Yeah, go on, feel your Boots.

- When my father started taking energy tablets, it affected our relationship.

- Glucose?

- No, if anything we drifted further apart.

My compass only points Southeast. It's downright awful.

Relocating cattle by hot air transport is very rare.

It happens once in a moo balloon.

A worker at the local butter factory was sick after sniffing some sour milk.

A colleague did the same and spewed.

The manager came over to investigate and he hurled also.

It was a churn reaction.

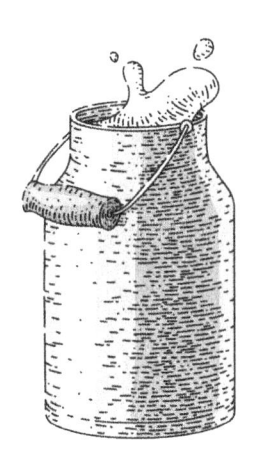

Heathrow use a giant set of scales to gauge the obesity of visitors from overseas.

It's foreigner weigh the best method.

I managed to find that actress Glenn, but not her missing racehorse.

Close, but no Shergar.

There's a bug going round that makes people impersonate cash registers.

It's ker-ching!

I'm sick of repeating my simple herbed grouse recipe.

I've told you thyme and ptarmigan.

My attempt at writing the world's shortest dictionary goes from strength to strength.

- Nintendo have made a game where Mario has a feeling of listlessness and dissatisfaction arising from a lack of occupation or excitement.

- Ennui?

- No, it's only available on Switch.

Benjamin Button's favourite games company is SEGA.

Scientists have designed a headset that allows you to play dice-based word games using telepathy.

The mind Boggles.

Does the Rotary Club offer spin classes?

My uncle was very happy working as a bus conductor, until he was hit by the No.37 during a big storm.

Went on a date with a woman who said she was a keen philatelist.
Turns out she was just a fan of stamps.

- Sister Sledge skidded on some Texan cow vomit and drove their Ford into a pit dug by highwaymen.

- Austin moo sick? Cortina trap?

- Yes. There was no turning back.

I know they're old-fashioned, but you can't beat a Filofax. Still the fastest way to send pastry.

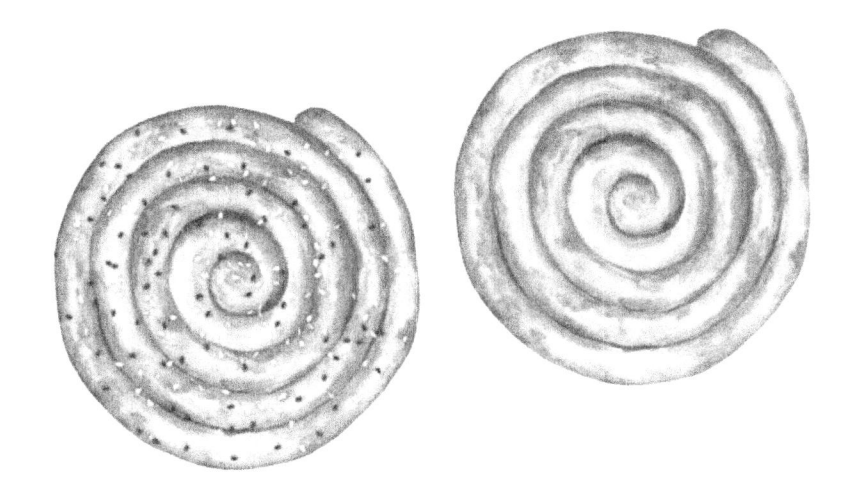

My friend felt better when she saw children dressed up as Rozonda Thomas, Tionne Watkins and Lisa "Left Eye" Lopes. Turns out she just needed a little TLC.

like to dress up as a pantomime cow for visitors, so if you come round I'll pop the cattle on.

- The boss tells me you've been promoted to head wildebeest shepherd.

- Yes, I herd the gnus.

Dedicated music teachers must make a concert ed effort.

- **Caller:** Can I speak to a Mrs Victoria-Cross Johnson?

- **Me:** Actually, my name is Angela. 'Victoria-Cross' is my medal name.

- Have you heard the new album by Ackroyd & DeVito?

- Nah, I'm not a fan of Dans' music.

Brass rubbing is a nice hobby until you get banned from the lingerie section in Marks & Spencer.

There's only one rowing machine at the local gym and people are always arguing over it.

I sold some Nostradamus-themed jewellery for inflated prices and got done for prophet earring.

Big show tout to my fellow ticket resellers!

- Just spoke to a man who tried to sell me an ice pack to hang around my dog's neck.

- Cold collar?

- No, I phoned him.

In Germany, when there aren't enough men to dig for coal, it is considered a mein herr setback.

Stevie Wonder used to employ me to make his hand garments, two days a week.
I was his part time glover.

My first celebrity crush was Meatloaf. He probably shouldn't have tried crowdsurfing.

My interview to be a dictator went so well, they hired me on despot.

When he got most nominations at the aquatic pet awards, I knew my seal was feted.

- I want an 11ft x 8ft bathroom in my Paris flat.

- Onze, huit?

- Yeah, next to the bedroom.

Saw some French doves driving a car.

It was a coupé.

There's a new show where bodybuilders crack walnuts with their biceps.

It's on Nutflex.

I know a proctologist who reckons he's so good he can do a DIY examination.

He's really up himself.

I won't listen to string quartets where the instruments are made of dumplings.

I hate acts of wonton violins.

Tour guides in Liverpool have responded to a pay cut by refusing to work. They're showing no Mersey.

My lounge isn't big enough to spin two animal pelts around at the same time.

Furs twirled problem.

Apparently you're not allowed to say that Hal went 'crazy' in 2001: A Space Odyssey

It's PC gone mad.

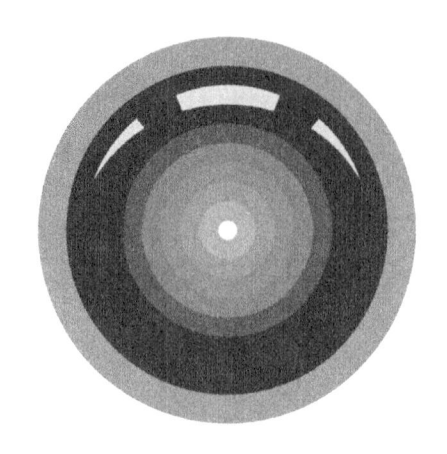

- When the government issues a new decree, I like to record it in writing.

- Diktat?

- No, in a notebook.

I often get criticised for working for the British Museum, but I'm past caring.

- I went to the monastery outfitters and there's a sign above the door that reads 'Caveat Emptor'.

- Buy abbeywear?

- I didn't know you spoke Latin.

Watched 'The Hunt For красный октябрь' last night.

It had Russian subtitles.

I met fellow fans of Star Wars skin art at a Tatooine convention.

I impress women by snoozing on dates.

It's my short kip display.

- My long-necked buddy messaged me to bet I wouldn't lie down behind the toilet door.

- Giraffe text loo dare?

- I did manage to block the breeze coming in a little, yes.

The Italian Job stunt drivers were denied a potential Oscar after they broke nominee rules.

Do blacksmiths study at FE college?

Making a human pyramid with my fellow traffic wardens was probably my finers' tower.

What comes after J in the Spanish alphabet.

Some say adding porridge to my morning cuppa is too much.

suppose it is oaty tea.

- I asked Pinnochio for a metal threaded fastener but he told me he didn't have any.

- No screw?

- I think he was telling the truth, actually.

I've removed all the travel sweets from my glovebox in an attempt to reduce my car bonbon footprint.

Apparently, there's a new trend for opaque crystal balls, but I can't see any future in them.

- I saw an old Olympic swimmer in the sea the other day.

- Goodhew?

- Yes, a lovely, pale azure.

My friend crossed the road to get some feathers out of a Flymo.

He got mown down.

When my dentist turned around, I saw his tail and realised he was actually a horse.

That was a real kick in the teeth.

When I agreed to be Dwayne Johnson's kinky slave, I knew I'd hit rock bottom.

I always wanted to captain a naval attack boat, but that ship assailed.

I don't overanalyse Carry On films. I take them at farce value.

As a forest ranger, I tend to spend Halloween tree core treating.

Scientists reckon that the average dog barks 23 times a day, but it's just a rrrrrough estimate.

I'm raising money to compete in the World Hide and Seek Championships, so I've set up a GoFindMe page.

Optimus Prime took a mechanics course after his therapist said he needed to work on himself.

A species of parasite has been discovered in the capital of Italy and been given the Latin name *Duranus Duranus*.

Because they're new Roman ticks.

I asked a Scottish farmer if he'd consider replacing his cattle prod with an electric guitar.

He said he preferred acoustic.

The museum thanked me for donating all my fossils, but I kept the aquatic dinosaur skeleton, so the plesiosaur was all mine.

Sorry.

Printed in Great Britain
by Amazon

54685003R00030